ENGINES at CORBY

Memories of an Industrious Railway System

Compiled by Peter Staughton

Reviving the memories of yesterday…

ISBN 978-1-915281-09-8

First published in 2024 by Transport Treasury Publishing Ltd., 16 Highworth Close, High Wycombe, HP13 7PJ

Turntable Publishing an imprint of Transport Treasury Publishing

Printed by Short Run Press Ltd., Exeter.

www.ttpublishing.co.uk

Front cover photos: In the late 1960's as the era of steam at the Corby Iron and Steel works was drawing to a close, the railway system was still operated by a large fleet of locomotives. One set, mostly painted in high visibility yellow, operated the iron, steel and tube works traffic. Another group of engines, painted in a more traditional green livery worked in the ironstone quarries travelling for several miles out into the countryside as they did so. This book is the author's personal record of these engines at work and the duties they undertook.

Back cover : A picture of a most treasured possession, the works plate from No. 20, a permanent reminder of good times spent at Corby watching a very busy railway at work.

Frontispiece: The development of the modern iron industry in Corby was prompted by the thick layer of ironstone that was revealed in the late 1870s during the construction of Corby Tunnel. It is clearly shown on the right hand side of the cutting wall in this 1960s picture of the southern portal of the tunnel. Since the time of this picture, not only has the vast steel making complex disappeared but the seam of ironstone is also hidden from view behind a mass of encroaching vegetation.

Bottom right : How the story begins, departing a waterlogged Earlstrees Quarry, No.44 *Conway* gets started with a delivery of iron ore bound for the works. Destined initially for the North Bank reception sidings, from there the ore will pass through the sinter plant, then in succession via the blast furnaces where it will be transformed into iron, to one of the steel making furnaces, the rolling mills and finally the tube works from whence it will emerge, at the southern outlet from the plant as fully manufactured lengths of tubing. What a transformation, from brown and grey lumps of nondescript rock to bright shiny steel tubes!

CONTENTS

1. INTRODUCTION

The decade that we refer to as the 1950s ended at midnight on the 31st December 1959 when I was 12 years old. To a youngster, everything in the world around me seemed to be stable and unchanging. The same old shops and businesses traded in our town, we travelled about on the same old buses, red within the Borough, green in the country, as we always had done so. The shoe factories carried on the traditions of previous generations, everyone drove British cars and our motorcycles were the envy of the world. Most reassuring was our local railway station which seemed permanent and everlasting. There was the same network of services managed by a familiar set of engines. That was the way it had been and that was the way I thought it would stay.

Fast forwards 10 short years through the 'swinging sixties' to 1970 and everything had altered, never to be the same again. Most relevant to our particular story is that the age of steam railways had effectively ended. The last regular services operated by steam on the national network finished in August 1968, and because of changing patterns in industry the use of steam locomotives, and indeed the use of industrial railways in general, also rapidly declined. From being so common that they barely merited a second glance, steam locomotives became a virtually extinct species and we assumed that once they were gone they would never return.

So during those 10 short years of the sixties, realising that the memories of what we were seeing before us would have to last a lifetime, many of us attempted to see as much working steam as we could, and hopefully take some half decent photographs to record the passing scene. For me a slightly grandiose ambition perhaps; a teenager with no money, limited photographic skills, concerned about 'O' Level GCE exams at school followed by getting a job, then establishing a career, with intense part time study at college as an extra. I could but hope and be optimistic.

As main line steam disappeared from our local area the interest turned to industrial railways, and the most interesting of those locally was the system at the Corby steelworks. This I became very familiar with over a number of years and it became the subject of many photographs. Finally working steam came to an end, but as is the way, life carried on. Eventually my collection of pictures was packed away, and over the next 55 or so years was moved from house to house, attic to attic, never quite forgotten but with always something more important taking precedence. It was only recently that I decided to fetch them down and sort through them. 55 years; a full half century and more. Would they have deteriorated? Would they be worth looking at? Do they match up with my rose tinted memories? Or will it all be a disappointment and with everything being consigned to the rubbish bin? In the event, sorting through them and selecting the more interesting ones has been a bittersweet experience. First thoughts were that I wished I had used a better camera and was more skilled at taking pictures. I should have been more adventurous and got around the works more than I did. But my pictures strongly reminded me of the very 'busy-ness' of the system, different engines, different trains, always something happening. So some of the more interesting ones are presented here,. I have tried to show just how active the railway system was and the scope of how it operated. I would ask readers to be a little indulgent. By the time everything was in place, career established, earning money, adequate holiday leave allowance, a reasonable camera and the appropriate skills to use it, steam at Corby had all but finished. But for those of you who knew Corby, I hope to relight some memories and for those of you who are unfamiliar with Corby,you will be able to see just what has passed.

2. TO SET THE SCENE

Ordnance Survey Map 133 from 1968 is representative of the area during the final years when steam was operational as it shows the extent of the iron and steel works and the main routes to the various quarry branches. Geographically the railway system extended from Oakley sidings in the southwest to the quarries at Harringworth in the north east, this was just over 8 miles. The route mileage of the actual tracks between these two places was of course many times this.

Most of the picture locations will be indicated on the original map but some of those specific to the photographs have been identified and shown in red text.

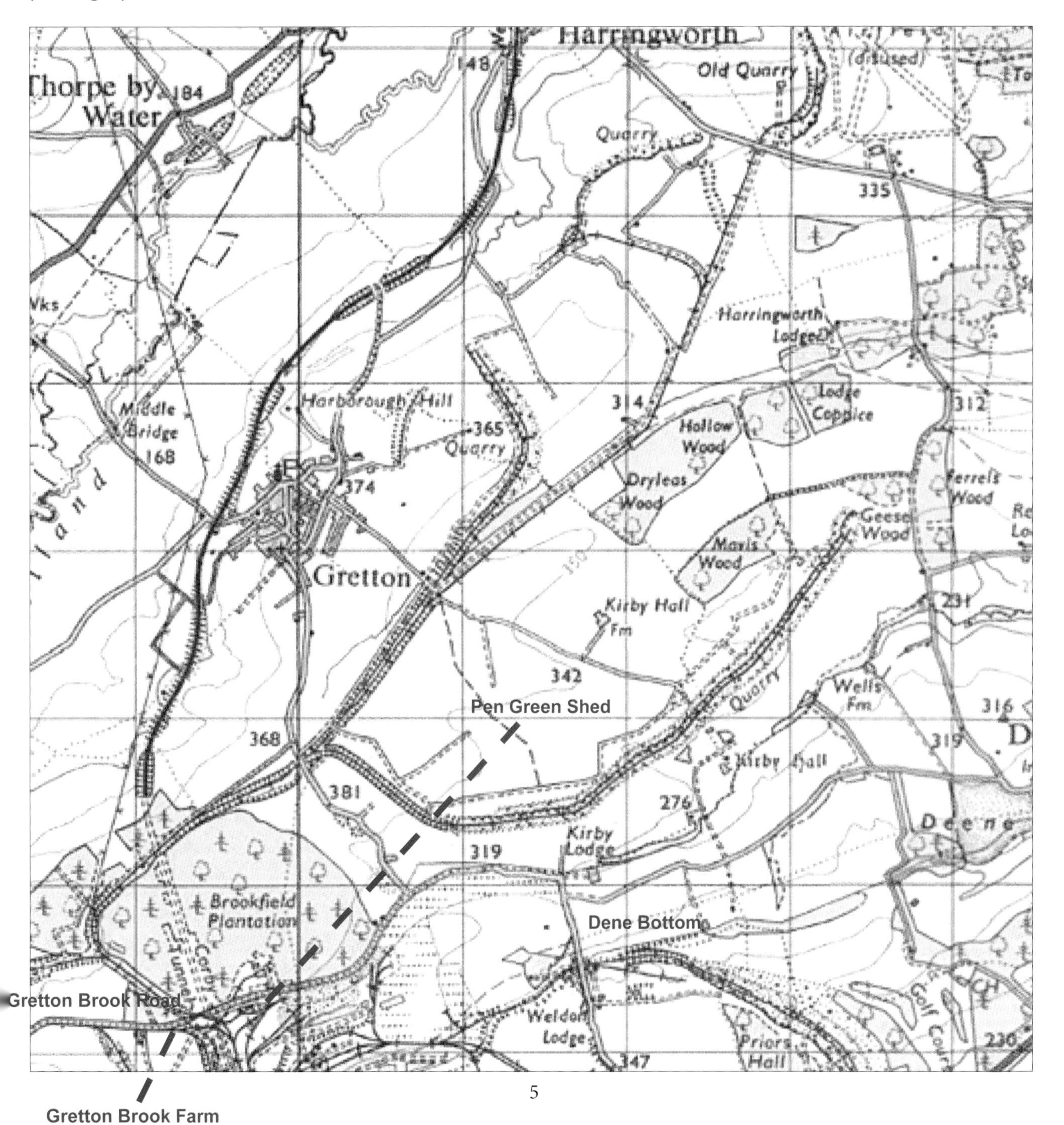

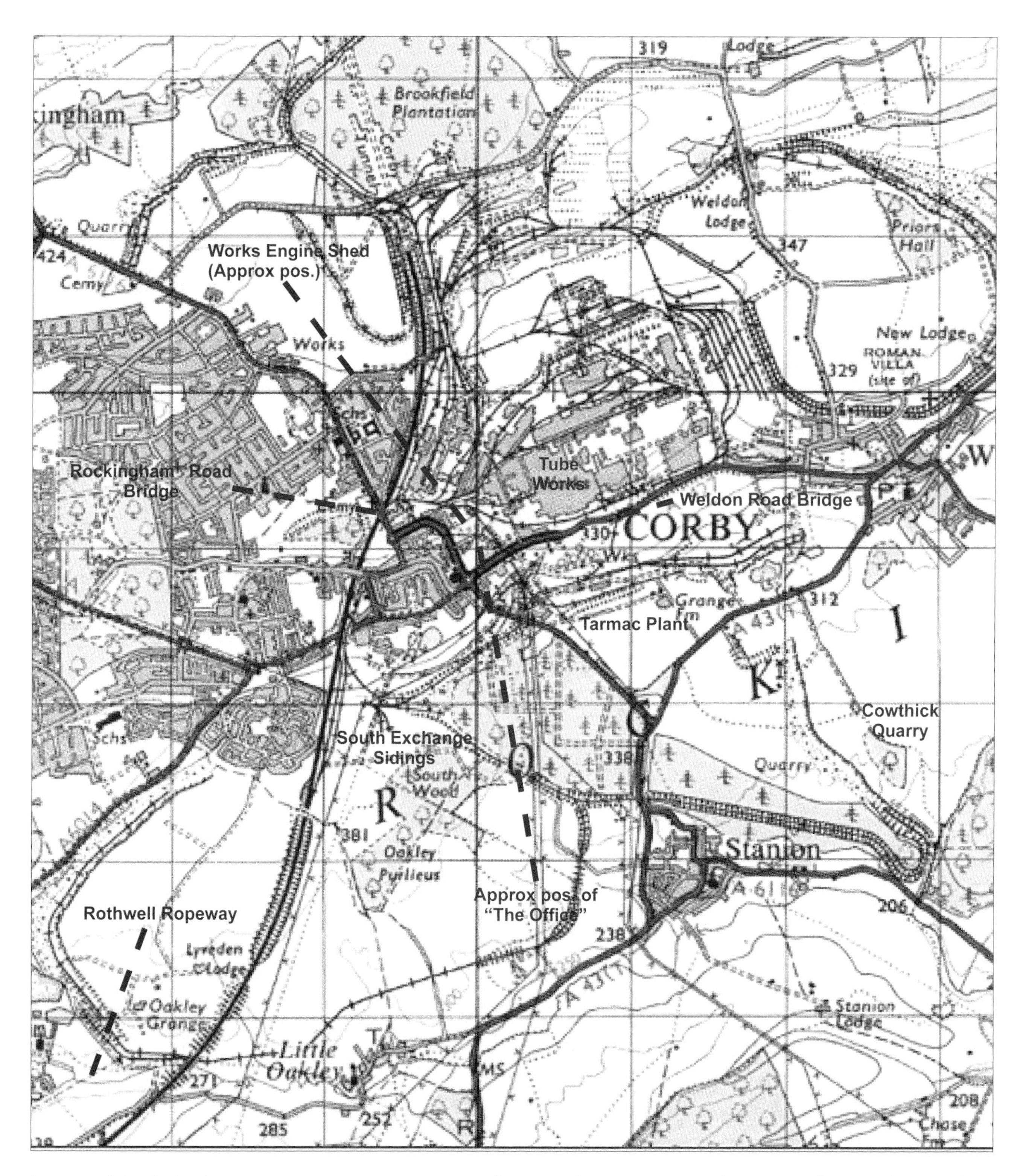

Unsurprisingly in the 50 or so years since we used to see the trains at Corby many changes have taken place. Much of the district has altered almost beyond recognition and the only section of railway that is still in use is the section from the south exchange sidings to the still functioning tube works. This also passes the former tarmac plant the site of which is still in use as a car storage depot.

3. ENGINES AT CORBY

During the time of my association with Corby, many of the older engines had gone and had been replaced by what would be regarded as fairly modern standardised designs.

The majority of engines used in the iron, steel and tube works were of a Hawthorn Leslie standard design with some later engines being constructed by their successors Robert Stephenson and Hawthorn, these were six coupled saddle tanks with outside 16 inch cylinders. Several of them had been converted to oil burning, my understanding being that the fuel was a by-product of the on-site coke ovens which would otherwise have gone to waste. One of the drivers mentioned that it was more like tar in consistency and to render it usable it required warming up to lower the viscosity. Fortuitously hot steam was more than sufficient to achieve this and of course on a steam railway there was always plenty of this available from one source or another including of course an engine's own boiler. All of the Hawthorns were painted in the safety canary yellow livery which looked very smart when newly applied. However the environment in the works and the lack of cleaning resulted in the paint either fading to a pale cream or darkening to almost black, with every shade imaginable in between. Another Hawthorn Leslie was No.33, a standard four wheeler, briefly used in the tube works before finding its way onto permanent way trains and eventually being transferred to Bromford Bridge tubeworks.

Additional to the Hawthorns was No.24, which for a time was regularly used in the tube works and was an example of the pre-austerity Hunslet tanks. There were also a small number of elderly Andrew Barclay standard 6 coupled saddle tanks which were used mainly on lighter duties, principally shunting the tarmac plant or on permanent way trains. One other old engine, another Barclay but 4 wheels coupled was No.26 which languished at the works shed for some time without ever turning a wheel before being taken away for scrap.

Although there was steam in abundance, the number of diesel locos, principally by English Electric, was slowly increasing, and as the older steam engines were taken out of service the Hawthorns, principally the oil fired ones, were cascaded down to take on their duties. It would be imagined that the engine drivers would be quite pleased to accept the better working environment associated with the diesels and I actually suggested this to one of the tube works drivers that he would no doubt be pleased when steam had finally finished. His response was quite unexpected, "Well, I'd miss the interest and with these things you can be here, there and everywhere at once," were his exact words. The significance of this became more obvious a few weeks later when I was observing some tube works shunting from our office window. Possibly something had caused an upset to the normal routine, and to put things right one of the Hawthorns spent a dramatic half an hour rapidly sprinting up and down from one end of the sidings to the other. 'Scurrying about' would hardly describe it, I honestly have never seen an industrial loco move so fast. First up to the top end, then hidden from view apart from the smoke, back down again, light engine but exhaust briefly roaring away, pick up three tube wagons, back up to the top again, push them up a different loop, back down, up to the top end, speed back down again, push more wagons up. And so it went on until the train was made up. It would never have been possible in the same timescale as a diesel.

Operations in the tube works sidings weren't helped by them being on a gradient. It was not unknown, especially when the rails were wet that when a train of loaded tube wagons was being moved in a downhill direction the engine brakes would be applied and the wheels would lock and the whole ensemble would go sliding along for a distance until it stopped. Possibly this was the reason for flats on the tyres and considering the proximity of an adjacent road crossing, a potential safety hazard. Fortunately providence always smiled and nothing ever actually came to grief although I would imagine that there were some occasional anxious moments on the footplate.

Most of those servicing the quarries were 6 wheeled saddle tanks by three different makers, Manning Wardle, Kitson, and Robert Stephenson and Hawthorn. However all were of a distinct

Entirely typical of the fleet of Hawthorn Leslies and looking tolerably clean is No.19, photographed in the south exchange sidings in 1966. This one is conventionally coal fired, the oil fired engines could be identified by the larger bunker that extended upwards between the cab rear windows and an external pipe that extended from the steam dome towards the cab.

lineage, being possessed of the raised water space above the firebox. From a distance the later Robert Stephenson engines, usually referred to as the '56' class, appeared very similar to the well known 'Austerity' type, but the difference was in the shorter saddle tanks, necessary because of the raised firebox. The exceptions were an outside cylindered Hudswell Clarke and a Manning Wardle, numbers No.39 and No.35 respectively. These engines with their smaller 15 inch cylinders were used exclusively on lighter jobs such as permanent way trains, duties which were later undertaken by the oldest of the larger Manning Wardles.

The top engines were the '56' class, with 18 inch cylinders and used for the hardest jobs. They looked the part too, with their squat chimneys, electric headlamps, squared off cabs and bunkers they exuded a real purposeful character. The sight and sound of a pair of these on a winters day, topping and tailing the last train of the day out of one of the pits was something to be remembered.

These minerals engines were all painted a sombre dark green livery with red rods and were usually kept very clean.

Another engine of interest was No.3 which was borrowed from Glendon East quarries for a time in 1967. This engine was a contemporary of No.24 one of the Hunslet "pre austerity" engines that were ordered for a projected railway to the quarries near Islip. According to Mr. Bates, the shed foreman at Pen Green, "they didn't need it and it required some work so we said we'd have it here". Whatever was wrong with it must have been rectified as on the couple of times that I saw it seemed to be working very effectively.

Diesel traction was also beginning to make an appearance in the quarries, 6 wheeled locomotives from Sentinels and a distinctive machine No.30, an eight coupled product of the Yorkshire Engine Company. For a time it was found regular use on the Oakley line, passing the tarmac plant whilst

At first glance it would be thought that No. 24 is another of the well known Hunslet designed Austerity saddle tanks, however it is one of a small number of engines specially designed for a proposed but aborted wartime extension of the Corby railway system to Islip quarries near Thrapston. These engines are known as the Hunslet '50550' class and it was from this design that the Austerity tanks were derived. In November 1967 it is seen here in the south exchange sidings having just arrived with a train from the tube works. The extended bunker to accommodate the oil fuel tanks can be clearly seen in this view. As this was the first of the batch of the '50550' type, should this engine be recognised as the progenitor of the many hundreds of Austerity tanks that were to follow?

No. 33 *Wellingborough* No.3 was transferred to Corby in 1963, following the closure of Wellingborough Ironworks. Initially it was used in the tube works and then allocated to the permanent way train. I used to see it quite often in its travels around the system but most frustratingly never had my camera with me whenever it appeared. Compared with the other engines at Corby, this Hawthorn Leslie was quite small and in early 1967 it was transferred to Bromford Bridge tube works in Birmingham where I at last managed to get a picture of it in January 1967.

doing so. Compared with the regular steam fleet its comings and goings were extremely understated, appearing to be completely indifferent to the nature of the gradient or indeed the load.

During my association with Corby No. 26 was the oldest engine on the site although I was never fortunate enough to see it working. There is however a modest drama associated with this picture which is still amusing to recall, even after more than half a century has elapsed. From the office window it was possible to see this engine outside the loco shed but it never seemed to move and to all intents and purposes it appeared to have no regular work to do. I mentioned this to one of the local enthusiasts and he was of the opinion that it was normally only ever used very infrequently. Except that one day, when looking out of the window for the regular Monday morning 'back at work shed perusal', it was obvious that it was no longer there. Later that day I happened to be in the works on 'official' business and noticed that the loco had been taken up to an on-site scrap yard. Clearly the end was in sight, if I wanted to get a picture of it then time was running out. So on the Friday evening of the same week I rode my motorcycle in through the tube works entrance

In November 1967, No.7 was one of the oldest engines on the Corby system and used as the Tarmac Plant shunter. As can be seen it is not in the best of condition and indeed has barely another year to go before being scrapped. Although shunting duties here were not particularly onerous, there always seemed to be something happening, trains of empty wagons being received, wagons being loaded under the crushing plant before being sorted and made into trains for onward dispatch. The shift finished late afternoon and from our office window it was possible to see the engine making its way slowly back up to shed, a welcome sign that going home time was fast approaching!

and up to the scrap yard. Although there was a labour dispute in the rolling mills the steel making plants were still functioning and all their products were being cast into ingots, about the size of a small car, and then taken up to the scrap yard for storage. On arrival there was a randomly stacked line of ingots, very many yards long and up to 10 feet high in places and No.26 was on the opposite side. The plan was to be in and out, so rather than trek down to the end I resolved to take a picture from a convenient ingot on the pile and then jump back down again. Once on a suitable ingot and composing a picture, for there were in fact two engines in the scrapyard, not one, I became aware of a faint burning smell and looking down saw that the soles of my motorcycle boots were actually smoking. Yes, the ingots were still hot, panic! A quick scramble down and the resulting picture is the result. The engine in the background is No. 34 *Callettwr* a sister engine of No. 35 which at that time was still in service.

Barclay No.26 in the scrap yard on the occasion of the 'smoking boots' referred to in the text, The engine in the background is what was left of No. 34.

No. 47 *Carnarvon* and No. 48 *Criggion*, near Pen Green shed, which can be seen in the background. Stewarts and Lloyds ordered a total of 15 of these engines between 1910 and 1941, initially from Manning Wardle and then from their successor firms, Kitsons and then Robert Stephensons and Hawthorns, surely a testament to their suitability for the job. Our little group of enthusiasts referred to them as "Kitsons" as a generic nickname since the original Manning Wardle examples were very much in a minority. They were all distinguished by the raised top fireboxes and, to see one of these boilers out of the frames, it had the appearance of a strange archaic hangover from the earliest days of railways. But they had been a feature of Manning Wardle construction for many years and were considered to be efficient steam generators. With tall, well shaped chimneys, these were well proportioned machines with a touch of an Edwardian elegance carried over from an earlier age and certainly not the average industrial ugly duckling. They were used all over the system, one of the typical jobs being to run empty wagons down into a quarry and position them as required for loading. Once this had been completed, one of the '56' class would arrive and the now loaded train would be topped and tailed out of the pit to the nearest adjacent set of sidings. Here the banker would separate from the train to collect another set of empties whilst the front engine would continue into the works reception sidings. However, in practice just about any engine permutation or combination seemed to happen and these engines often managed quite heavy trains into the works on their own account.

Photographed at the same time as the two Kitsons was No. 64, the last steam loco to be built for the Corby system in 1958 by Robert Stephensons and Hawthorns at their Newcastle works. These engines, usually referred to as the '56' class, were ordered as a consequence of the extension of the works railway system to Harringworth quarries and although very effective machines, in the preservation era they have acquired the unfortunate and universal nickname of 'Uglies'. Compared with the earlier engines these have 18 inch cylinders but still retain the raised top firebox. They were also equipped with a turbo electric generator, electric lighting, and were fitted with a radio set for use in conjunction with the first aid and rescue train.

No.39 *Rhos* was very much the odd engine out in the minerals fleet and was only used on works and permanent way trains. It was usually very busy, so to see it apparently dumped out of use at Pen Green in November 1968 was quite a surprise. Fortunately it escaped the scrapman's torch and has since been preserved.

ENGINES at CORBY

No.	Name	Type	Cylinders	Builder	Works No./Year
6		0-6-0ST	O/C	AB	1242/11
7		0-6-0ST	O/C	AB	1268/12
11		0-6-0ST	O/C	HL	3824/34
12		0-6-0ST	O/C	HL	3825/34
13		0-6-0ST	O/C	HL	3826/34
14		0-6-0ST	O/C	HL	3827/34
15		0-6-0ST	O/C	HL	3836/34
16		0-6-0ST	O/C	HL	3837/34
18		0-6-0ST	O/C	HL	3896/36
19		0-6-0ST	O/C	HL	3889/36
20		0-6-0ST	O/C	HL	3897/36
21		0-6-0ST	O/C	HL	3931/37
22		0-6-0ST	O/C	RSHN	6944/40
23		0-6-0ST	O/C	RSHN	7025/41
24		0-6-0ST	I/C	HE	2411/41
26		0-4-0ST	O/C	AB	678/90
29		0-6-0ST	O/C	AB	1457/15
32		0-6-0ST	O/C	HL	3888/36
33	WELLINGBORO' No.3	0-4-0ST	O/C	HL	3813/35
34		0-6-0ST	I/C	MW	1316/95
35		0-6-0ST	I/C	MW	1317/95
38	DOLOBRAN	0-6-0ST	I/C	MW	1762/10
39	RHOS	0-6-0ST	O/C	HC	1308/19
40		0-6-0ST	O/C	HL	3375/19
41	RHYL	0-6-0ST	I/C	MW	2009/21
44	CONWAY	0-6-0ST	I/C	K	5469/33
45	COLWYN	0-6-0ST	I/C	K	5470/33
46	CARDIGAN	0-6-0ST	I/C	K	5473/33
47	CARNARVON	0-6-0ST	I/C	K	5474/33
48	CRIGGION	0-6-0ST	I/C	K	5476/36
52		0-6-0ST	I/C	RSHN	7004/40
53		0-6-0ST	I/C	RSHN	7030/41
54		0-6-0ST	I/C	RSHN	7031/41
56		0-6-0ST	I/C	RSHN	7667/50
57		0-6-0ST	I/C	RSHN	7668/50
58		0-6-0ST	I/C	RSHN	7669/50
59		0-6-0ST	I/C	RSHN	7670/50
61		0-6-0ST	I/C	RSHN	7672/50
62		0-6-0ST	I/C	RSHN	7673/50
63		0-6-0ST	I/C	RSHN	7761/54
64		0-6-0ST	I/C	RSHN	8050/58
3	No. 80	0-6-0ST	I/C	HE	2417/41

Opposite is a list of locomotives that worked at Corby during the final years of steam.

Engines shown with shaded numbers are the ones from the iron and steelworks fleet that were oil-fired.

Key to builders names above:

AB	Andrew Barclay, Sons & Co. Ltd	Kilmarnock
HC	Hudswell Clarke & Co Ltd.	Leeds
HE	Hunslet Engine Co. Ltd	Leeds
RSHN	Robert Stephenson & Hawthorns Ltd.	Newcastle
HL	Hawthorn Leslie & Co Ltd	Newcastle
K	Kitson & Co. Ltd	Leeds
MW	Manning Wardle & Co Ltd	Leeds

4. CORBY WORKS

Most of my early railway enthusiast journeys involved pedal cycles and were perforce restricted to locations quite close to home, so my first ever visit to Corby on the 18th May 1964, using my newly acquired motorcycle, seemed both a blissfully effortless but nevertheless adventurous experience, one that was destined never to be forgotten and indeed it was the first of many.

Later, whilst attending a new employees induction session at the Stewarts and Lloyds Corby steelworks in 1965 we were proudly informed that we were now working at "one of the largest integrated steelworks in Europe". As our guide explained, "iron ore comes in, tubes go out." Everything else that happened in between these two events occurred within the confines of the works, the perimeter of which, depending on how exactly it was measured, was about 5 miles. To source the iron ore, a network of railway lines extended out into the surrounding countryside, some of these being several miles long, and in the works itself almost every part of the production process required some sort of rail transport.

Many years later I recall reading that the system at Corby was one of the largest privately owned ones in the country. This was quite believable and to manage all the various types of traffic approximately 40 engines were available, divided into two separate allocations. Working out from a large modern shed at Pen Green, on the northern side of Corby, were the ironstone quarry engines which were owned by a subsidiary, 'S & L Minerals Ltd' and were in a dark green livery. These were almost exclusively steam, but augmented by a small number of diesels including some on trial

No. 24 is seen cautiously moving through the works with a train of vans in October 1969. This section of the railway network was also very busy and fortuitously a footpath passed alongside the boundary fence allowing pictures to be taken.

Two views from our office window of part of the Corby complex. The upper view dating from June 1968 shows the four blast furnaces in the background. The three tall chimneys are part of the Glebe coke ovens. The tower immediately to their left was used to quench the hot coke after it had been removed from the coking oven. Prominent in the middle ground is the works engine shed with three of the Hawthorn Leslies awaiting their next turn of duty. To the left of the engine shed are the wagon shops where extensive repairs were carried out. The lower picture shows all five coke oven chimneys. In front of them is the Bessemer shed and in the right background one of the steel making plants. This picture dates from December 1967. The steam in the centre emanates from shunting operations in the loco shed. Several engines can be seen, one of which is No.24.

from Rolls Royce, and all were stabled at Pen Green. Serving the iron, steel and tube works was a separate fleet of engines, mixed steam and diesel, most of which were painted in a canary yellow high visibility livery and lettered 'S & L'. Many of these engines were operated continually on a 3 shift 24 hour basis and in the normal course of their duties often worked from stabling points around the works, returning to their separate shed located within the works only when necessary.

Photography inside the works, even for an employee of the firm, was not easy but fortunately there were plenty of places around the periphery where locomotives could be seen at work. And as I was there during the working day it was possible to observe some of the train operating patterns and work out suitable lineside locations. Also, the minerals engines worked a Saturday morning shift and ownership of the motorcycle was most useful as it was possible to venture out into the countryside back lanes where there were a number of road overbridges. With judicious timing and depending upon which quarries were actually being worked, see some of the inbound loaded iron ore trains. On such days we would always finish up at Pen Green shed where it was possible to see the last of the inbound trains passing by and then observe the engines as they finished for the day and one by one were disposed of and put back on shed.

Although my time as an employee was of relatively short duration the connection with the railways at Corby was maintained until steam was finally phased out in the early 1970s. My memories are of a busy, extensive, and efficient railway system that handled a wide variety of different traffics. Its engines were often worked extremely hard and must have paid for themselves many times over.

During March 1969 No.14 is seen passing through the works with a train of hopper wagons.

A murky November day in 1968 saw No. 18 slowly moving through the works with a rail mounted crane made by Smith's of Rodley near Leeds. This machine was used very extensively for track maintenance and appears in several of my photographs.

No. 21 passes by in March 1969. It appears to have lost its number plate with the numerals being painted on, according to my notes this engine was one of the tube works shunters at this time. In the distance can be seen one of the ubiquitous English Electric diesels.

The works shed was not as impressive as its Pen Green counterpart. The number of engines "on shed" at any one time was quite small as most engines were stabled out on the job in the works. In the upper picture are a number of Hawthorns, most of which are in steam, and in the lower one some building work appears to be in progress with just one of the Hawthorns and No. 24 in view.

The permanent way train was liable to show up anywhere and here it is seen with No. 12 in October 1968, once again a fortuitous picture through the fence from the footpath. The van on the end of the train was an ex-British Railways six wheeler. In the background two of the blast furnaces are visible and also the bases of a couple of the Glebe coke oven chimneys, but most noticeable is part of the complex network of elevated pipes that were such a characteristic feature of the place, wherever one went it was always beneath a canopy of pipes. April 1971 as the era of steam at Corby was coming to an end, shrouded in steam and smoke.

No.22 is captured whilst passing through the works.

5. ROCKINGHAM ROAD

The Rockingham Road Bridge in Corby overlooked the northern exchange sidings, 'Lloyds Ironstone Sidings', and the access tracks to the blast furnace area. When the furnaces were being tapped, molten iron and molten slag were collected and delivered by train to their respective destinations. Iron was destined for one of the various steel making processes and slag for the tarmac plant where it was ultimately used in the manufacture of road making materials. Ironically the attendant in the adjacent clocking-in office referred to these operations as 'snapping up' but in fact shunting movements with these trains were slow and deliberate as clearly any sort of derailment involving searing hot liquid metal or slag could have quite serious consequences. Engines would draw a train down from the furnaces into a head shunt that terminated adjacent to the Rockingham Road bridge, then would reverse direction and slowly push the train towards the works. The molten iron trains typically comprised 3 or 4 of the special ladle wagons and proceeded at a very sedate pace until they disappeared from view into the works. From the furnaces the slag was run into open topped 4 wheeled tipping wagons and when freshly tapped would be red hot and extremely fluid, to such an extent that it could be seen literally sploshing about just beneath the rim of the wagon. This material would then be disposed of by taking it to the slag bank which was

No.14 is pictured in June 1969 returning a set of empty ladle wagons used for transporting molten metal to the blast furnaces. The furnaces themselves were situated behind the "Stewarts and Lloyds Limited Corby" canopy, beneath which the metal and slag were run off and transferred to the appropriate wagons. When full, loaded ladle wagons would be slowly brought down from the furnace area, then would briefly halt before reversing direction towards the steelworks and being slowly propelled into the appropriate steel making plant. The ladle would then be lifted off the wagon chassis and carried over to the processing plant where it would be slowly inverted and its contents emptied. I only ever witnessed this once or twice and it was a sight never to be forgotten, even if it was all in a day's work for the men concerned. To the left is the then still busy Kettering to Manton railway which passed through Corby Tunnel and also over the Welland Viaduct, near Harringworth, the longest masonry viaduct in the country.

just over a mile away, a duty undertaken by the English Electric diesels. Clearly it was desirable to tip the slag whilst it was still molten and before it solidified so these trains travelled at more normal speeds. Depending on the number of operational furnaces there would be a fairly regular service to and from the slag bank using a direct route that passed under the Corby to Weldon Road near to what is now referred to as 'The Lodge'. As a bonus all the shunting operations just mentioned were of course duplicated because the empty trains had to be returned to the furnaces and additionally there was transfer traffic to and from the main line, British Railways as it was then.

A characteristically busy scene taken from the Rockingham road bridge with No.54 seen shunting a train of three ladle wagons. This engine was one of the S. & L. Minerals fleet and was presumably on loan to the ironworks because of an engine shortage. The engine on the right of the picture is No.29, pushing a train of slag wagons.

On the same day, two pictures of No. 29 with a set of empty slag tipping wagons. This engine was another of the elderly Andrew Barclays and it was the only time I saw it working as it was withdrawn from service the following year.

November 1968 and I was fortunate enough to see No. 32 at work as steam activity was by then quite reduced, partly due to the arrival of the ex-Oxfordshire Ironstone diesels, one of which was busy at work in the background. The inverted hopper wagon seen just behind the engine must have suffered a substantial misfortune for it to have been removed from the rails and inverted in such a manner.

The steepness of the gradient of the tracks leading up to the furnaces can be readily appreciated in this picture as No.12 runs downhill with a short train. One of the Oxfordshire Ironstone diesels is also seen just intruding into the picture, its Corby surroundings being very different from those at Wroxton. April 1969.

April 1967 and No.32 propels a lengthy train of slag wagons.

No. 15 on the 18th May 1964 with a train of ladles.

14th April 1967 and a general view from Rockingham Road bridge with No. 14 with a short train of slag wagons. One of the English Electric diesels can be seen in the centre of the picture awaiting its next job and in the background what appears to be another train of slag tippers is being propelled up to the furnaces. It is noteworthy that all of the Hawthorn Leslies seen in this selection of pictures working in the ironworks are all of the non-coal fired variety.

6. THE TUBE WORKS

From 1965 to 1968 I worked for Stewarts & Lloyds Ltd at Corby Iron and Steel Works. My new office directly overlooked the Tube Works marshalling sidings, and from other parts of the building it was possible to see a further considerable area of the works. Not surprisingly, I took a keen interest in the railway system. In 1965 one of the three locomotives regularly employed in the Tube Works worked on a day shift basis. The other two were on twenty-four hour duties, and I will deal with these first.

One locomotive was continually engaged in collecting loaded wagons from various loading bays in the Tube Works and working them to the marshalling sidings. These were about half-a-mile long and at their widest consisted of about six loops and five dead end roads. The other engine would take these loaded tube wagons to the South Exchange sidings, about 2¼ miles away. The tube works sidings were not continually busy; after about 2½ hours shunting the engines were idle for a similar period whilst wagons were loaded. Before the start of a shunting session the crews – each engine in the Tube Works carried a crew of three: a driver and two shunters – would spend some time preparing the engines. This often involved shovelling mountains of ash out of the smokebox as well as the more usual jobs of oiling the motion, filling the tank, and making up the fire. Whilst steam was being raised, engines would have the blowers on, shooting black columns of smoke into the sky. Sometimes it was necessary to return an engine to the shed, either to coal up or to exchange it for another one. One engine would start sorting wagons to be taken to the South Sidings, whilst the other would go around the Tube Works picking up full wagons and returning the empties. Each loading bay had one or more roads served by an overhead travelling crane. The locomotive ran in light pulled out the full wagons, pushed in some empties, and then ran out light again. Most of the tubes were loaded into 22 ton long wheelbase tube wagons but there was a fair

A view from the office window, it wasn't all tube trains as this picture of No. 19 with a short train of tank wagons shows. Further up the siding can be seen some larger, more modern tank wagons, so quite possibly they are a new delivery with the older, smaller wagons being in the process of being collected. Not the best quality picture but worth including for its subject matter. 1966.

Two pictures of operations near the tube works road bridge. In June 1967 No. 15 is passing through with the Smith crane and permanent way train. This particular engine was quite frequently allocated to this duty.

As seen from Weldon Road, No. 12 arrives at the tube works from the south exchange sidings with a delivery of empty tube wagons. 19th April 1967.

The Smith's crane (again) being propelled through the works by No.19. When not in use, in between shunting sessions, engines were stabled on the two tracks leading up to the highly visible shuttered door. A water supply was provided here which can just be seen to the right of the door.

proportion of bogie bolsters. Some of the loading bays were at right angles to the general direction of the sidings and were entered by sharp curves. Most of these were checkrailed but some were laid in grooved tramway type rail.

A full train having been marshalled, the train loco would set it back in the direction of Weldon, under the Tube Works access road and onto a long loop where there was a weighbridge. Wagons were sometimes weighed on this but I imagine that the tubes would be weighed before leaving the works. From here the train moved forwards on to the main line, running on the wrong line for a few yards before crossing over to the correct left hand side. After passing again under the access road and down a steep bank, the descent continued under Weldon Road bridge and towards the Tarmac Plant. Past this plant, near the Stanion Lane bridge, the regulator would be opened for the climb to the South Sidings. This was quite a tough proposition for the Hawthorn Leslies since trains might have as many as thirty wagons and occasionally even more sometimes enginemen were able to solicit the help of another loco returning downhill light.

From our office it was possible to see trains going down as far as the Tarmac Plant. In the cutting beyond we could follow their progress by the sight of their exhausts. About a quarter-of-a-mile after Stanion Lane bridge the Minerals branch to Cowthick and Oakley Ironstone Pits diverged to the left; a little further on was a dump for old wagons, after which the South Sidings could be seen. The gradient steepened in the last few hundred yards and in addition there was a very sharp right hand curve. Locos sometimes stalled on this and the train had to be divided. As the line at the South Sidings ended in a headshunt, full trains had to be set back into the BR exchange sidings proper. Having collected empties and pulled them into the headshunt, the engine ran round and coupled onto the front before setting off for the works; all this was done quite smartly. Depending on the water situation, a stop might be made opposite the Tarmac Plant to fill up on the return journey. Meanwhile the other engine would have marshalled another train ready to take away. The fresh empties would be distributed or left in sidings whilst another load was taken down to the BR sidings. Each round trip took about 45

Approaching the south exchange sidings is No.16 with a loaded tube train in February 1968. The tops of the Glebe coke oven chimneys are just visible in the background.

minutes with two or three trips being made in quick succession.

Another regular job done by one of the Tube Works shunters was the collection early in the afternoon of the oil tank wagons that supplied fuel for the Tube Works furnaces. In 1965 these trains consisted of about five S&L internal-user wooden-framed tankers. (By the end of 1967 two long wheelbase SHELL-BP tankers formed the train; by 1968 it was down to a single bogie tanker which rather dwarfed the locomotive.) Often permanent way trains would pass by the offices, or do some work in the vicinity. These were usually powered by one of the two Barclay six-coupled saddle tanks, Nos. 6 or 7. When these had gone four-coupled saddle tank No.33 *Wellingborough* No.3 (Hawthorn Leslie 3813 of 1935) was the regular engine, and after that one of the big Hawthorns. For a short time the Minerals Department permanent way train was a regular visitor, powered by No. 39 *Rhos*. The restrained comings and goings of this Hudswell Clarke were in direct contrast to those of the vociferous Hawthorns.

There were also the out-of-course events that occur on any busy railway system. About once a month the breakdown crane was passed through on some errand. Once a Hawthorn came chuffing through with ten hot slag wagons, and on one occasion a huge gearwheel was propelled through on a flat wagon at a speed less than walking pace. I sometimes had to go to the research laboratories which also overlooked the sidings, and one day a permanent way gang was outside removing a couple of sidings with Barclay loco 6 and about seven flat wagons. A ganger called the train forward so that lifted rails could be loaded up and taken away. The driver was a little inattentive; he missed the signal to stop and was alarmed to see the first two wagons run off the end of the rails and bounce over the sleepers. Putting the engine in reverse, he tried to pull them back on again, but this was more than the Barclay could do. The wagons were uncoupled and left behind to be dealt with by a crane several days later.

Earlier on I mentioned the day shift engine. This had to work a line – we called it the 'centre road' – that ran into the Electrical Resistance Weld (ERW) Plant. Its particular job involved pulling loaded wagons out of the loading bay and taking them up towards the Blast Furnace area. After running

No.24 was very much the odd engine out amongst the collection of Hawthorns and Barclays that were its contemporaries. Nevertheless its size and extra power rendered it most suitable for tube works duties and, indeed, during my time at Corby it was so employed for many months at a time. These two pictures were taken near the south exchange sidings in November 1967 and Corby North signal box can be seen in the distance. I have particular cause to remember these pictures as the driver offered me a footplate ride back to the tube works. To my everlasting regret I had to decline because not only had I left a borrowed motorcycle parked by the main road but this was a lunch time visit and my interest in looking out of the office window at passing locomotives had been noticed by those on high, best not to chance it!

Even steam locomotives can be cold when there is a stiff winter breeze blowing through the cab but the work still goes on. A study in concentration as the driver of No. 13 executes shunting operations in the South Exchange Sidings. December 1967.

forward it deposited them in a siding to await collection by one of the other Tube Works engines. The loco then returned to the ERW Plant with empty wagons. In 1965 the regular engine for this job was *Wellingborough* No.3 which was painted in the standard yellow 'safety' livery and looked very smart when clean. At first its nameplates were painted black but later the letters were picked out in cream paint. The engine made several trips a day, but most of the time it stood in a siding just outside the ERW Plant, sometimes going to the shed for water; it finally retired there about 4pm each day. The centre road crossed one of the main entrances into the works by a level crossing and on one side of this the track foundations were a little soft so that locos would bump either up or down with a noticeable lurch. The six wheelers didn't suffer too badly but *Wellingborough* No.3 came over the crossing rather like a pram being bumped over a kerb, to the amusement of even non-railway minded onlookers.

The normal load of fourteen wagons proved almost too much for *Wellingborough* No.3 even on a dry day. If wet, this engine would begin to lose its grip just beyond the level crossing and take fifteen minutes to slip and slither the next hundred yards. During this time the level crossing would be blocked, resulting in disruption of vehicular and pedestrian traffic. A six coupled Hawthorn eventually took over, but shortly afterwards this regular engine duty was abolished and one of the twenty-four hour engines went over several times a day. This left *Wellingborough* No.3 without a job. For a time it was a regular permanent way engine; it was really too small for any other work and was eventually transferred to the company's Bromford Bridge Tube Works in January 1967.

In 1965 it was usual for two engines to cover the twenty-four hour duties for several weeks at a time, only going to the shed for washouts or refuelling. Certain engines seemed to be regulars whilst others appeared very infrequently. In 1965 I remember Hawthorns 19 and 20 being used for some time, then Hawthorns 20 and 21 for a lengthy period. Another favourite was Hunslet

A footplate view from No. 16 just arriving at the south exchange sidings with a very long train of loaded tubes receding into the distance. February 1968.

No.24, which was bigger than the Hawthorns and was no doubt considered more suitable. It used to work for about six weeks, disappear for a little while and then return again. By the end of 1966 this engine was in a poor state, indicated by the numerous clanks, knocks and bangs from the motion. At one time her whistle developed a habit of sticking open which was rather awkward when approaching level crossing gates. No.24 usually managed two of the necessary four toots; then the whistle would stick open until the driver had climbed up the tank and given it the big hammer treatment. Oil-fired engines were not favoured at first although 18 and 16 had fairly long spells on these duties. I understand that the excessive exhaust fumes from the oil-burners precluded their general use on jobs that entailed frequent entering of covered areas such as at the Tube Works. By the end of 1968 locomotives were changed every two or three days and, as far as I know, No.23 was the only engine not used on Tube Works duties during the period under discussion. 'Rare' engines were Nos.12 and 32, usually to be found around the Blast Furnace area, and No.40, which did a few days in March and June 1967, its regular job being to work the Lime Plant.

By February 1970, the Tube Works duties were completely dieselised. Steam locomotives were things of the past.

The above was originally published in the 'Industrial Railway Record' in June 1971.

One of my pals at Corby was quite friendly with some of the tube works engine drivers and he was quite adept at persuading them to let us have occasional footplate trips. These engines normally had a crew of three, a driver and two shunters, so it can be imagined that it was quite a squeeze with five of us on the footplate. Fortuitously the engines upon which we rode were all oil burning ones because there would have been absolutely no room to swing a coal shovel should that have been necessary. A ride on the typical industrial loco could hardly be described as restful but on my the first trip I was surprised how much extra noise there was on the footplate, even when coasting downgrade. Flats on the wheels caused the cab to rattle and vibrate, there was a rhythmic banging emanating from a worn reversing lever quadrant, and to add to it all there was a deep humming in the background from the burner. Once we started working against the gradient, the regulator was opened and the reversing lever pulled over, the aural experience could perhaps be described as rather intense.

On one particular trip with a loaded tube train we hadn't gone very far before it became apparent that the engine was struggling, our pace began to noticeably slow and there were doubts as to how far up the gradient we would actually get. Fortunately one of the English Electric diesels was returning down the bank from the exchange sidings light engine and our driver energetically attracted their attention by leaning out of the cab and punching his left fist into his cupped right hand, obviously a signal for a push. This was not a completely straightforward operation as the potential helper had to continue on its own track until it encountered a crossover, then reverse direction, and hopefully be able to catch our train up. For the next few minutes the discussion on the footplate was about whether the other driver had got the message, "is he on, or not?" Meanwhile our Hawthorn was gamely hanging on, but our speed slowed right down to a walking pace. The length of our train made it quite impossible to ascertain whether we were actually getting a push, but the final consensus was that we were indeed being banked by the diesel and we eventually made it to the south exchange sidings with our train. But all in a days work and enacted with what can be described as a nonchalant sangfroid.

On yet another trip we weren't so lucky, and our train stalled halfway around the curve just short of our destination in the sidings. Our driver turned the fire up to maximum whilst the shunters went off to pin the brakes down in the back half of the train before it could be divided, leaving me and my pal on the footplate. There was a strong easterly breeze blowing and the black smoke from our chimney was carried over to an adjacent housing estate where, as it happened, there was a considerable amount of pristine white washing hanging out to dry. Judging from the sentiments of the comments from the upstairs windows our stalled smoky, sooty steam locomotive wasn't exactly flavour of the month!

Worse was to follow. By the time our driver decided there was enough steam for a restart the two shunters were still busy and hadn't returned. My pal, keen to assist, rode on the engine so as to be able to act as a pointsman when required. The front part of the train was then drawn forwards into a headshunt ready to be set back into the exchange sidings. My pal climbed down, threw the point lever, ran back, clambered up the engine footsteps and slipped. His ankle was right under the circumference of the rear driving wheel of the engine. Fortunately our driver was alert, sensing something he turned around, saw what had happened, snapped the brake on and disaster was averted. It was all over in seconds and although no harm was done it was a chilling reminder that we were actually in a potentially hazardous work environment. Of all the various incidents that we experienced over the years whilst riding on engines this was definitely the most potentially serious. All in all quite a memorable Saturday afternoon!

The events described above certainly weren't everyday occurrences. When I was looking out of the office window, or was down by the Tarmac Plant and on other trips that we participated in all the operations seemed to work with a practised routine efficiency. Day in, day out, empty wagons came in, full ones were taken out, all with a continuous high degree of reliability.

Another picture from the office window, December 1967, and tube works stalwart No.20 is seen during shunting operations.

7. THE TARMAC PLANT

One of the busiest sections of the whole system was adjacent to the tarmac plant which was situated adjacent to Stanion Lane, a short distance to the south of Corby. Here molten blast furnace slag was tipped and cooled before being made into a durable road surfacing material. It had its own dedicated shunting loco which worked a day shift but the main interest here was the double tracked line that connected the British Railways south exchange sidings, adjacent to 'Corby North' signal box, with the works. This was used by tube works trains for deliveries and empty wagon collections and also by iron ore trains via branches connecting Cowthick and Oakley quarries, these latter being in the charge of the engines based at Pen Green. From the Oakley quarry sidings there was also an overhead cableway connection to quarries at

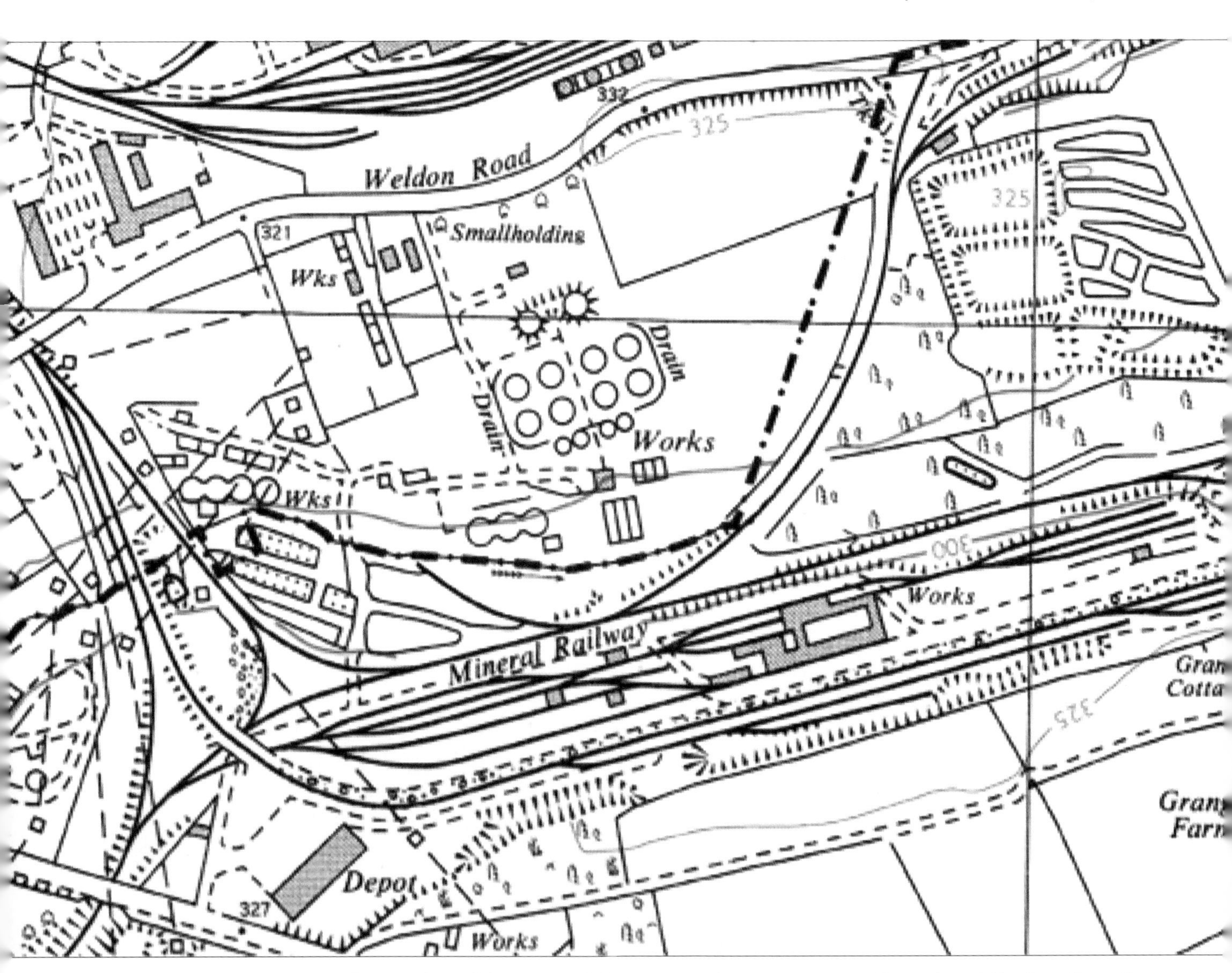

No signal boxes here. The section of line around the tarmac plant was very well used and the location of several closely spaced junctions and crossings. All the points were hand worked from adjacent point levers and safety was entirely down to the vigilance of the loco crews. This 1971 Ordnance Survey map shows the general track layout but somewhat simplified. The flyover used by the slag trains is clearly shown and the two bridges passing beneath Weldon Road, the sidings beyond are part of the tube works complex. Stanion Lane bridge is at the bottom left. Two water towers were located approximately adjacent to the 'e' in 'Mineral Railway'. Our office building is indicated on the map by a red spot, much time was spent looking out of the windows.

Rothwell and when operational this too created extra traffic. Leaving the exchange sidings there was a steep gradient down as far as Stanion Lane bridge followed by a short level section passing the Tarmac Plant before the line climbed up to a bridge passing under Weldon Road and accessing the tube works sidings. Iron ore trains continued past the tube works to their final destination at the North Bank reception sidings. An added interest adjacent to the tarmac plant was a pair of water towers and depending upon the circumstances, trains that stopped here often faced a challenging restart as there was a substantial uphill climb in either direction.

Blast furnace slag was bought down from the iron works furnaces, crossing over the double tracked 'main line' by a flyover and then continuing on an embankment to the slag bank itself where it was tipped. This was a regular 7 days a week occurrence with added impact after nightfall because when a wagon was tipped there would be a brief vivid flash followed by streams of bright orange and red running down the side of the slag bank. Even when viewed from a distance it was most awe inspiring. However slag tipping didn't always go to plan and sometimes it was necessary to vigorously rough shunt and bang the wagons about before a semi solid mass weighing several tons could be persuaded to separate from the tipping wagon body and go tumbling down the side of the slag bank.

A clean No.22 passes out from under Stanion Lane and sets off to return to the Iron and Steel works area. August 1967.

I was never able to photograph this at Corby but the attached photograph from the slag bank at an ironworks in Staffordshire captures the event perfectly, first the flash and then a wave of heat. Drama indeed! It seemed that there was always something happening down there, imagine an industrial Clapham Junction, and I spent many happy hours amongst the grime, the grit, and the smoke, truly an industrial railway enthusiast paradise.

The shunting duties at the tarmac plant were not particularly onerous and during my early visits one of the old Andrew Barclays, either No.6 or No.7 was assigned to this task. These were amongst the very oldest engines still working at Corby and indeed the seemed to have crews to match as one of the regular drivers on this job was referred to as 'Old Pete'. Nevertheless, the work seemed to agree with him as he always seemed very happy and cheerful. Once tipped and cooled, the slag was transferred to a crushing plant with final onwards transportation in the ubiquitous 16 ton mineral wagons. Shunting operations usually finished about 4 o'clock in the afternoon and it was always a welcome sight from our office window to see the old Barclay shuffling back up to the shed at not much more than a walking pace on just a breath of steam.

On another lunchtime visit the tarmac plant shunting engine was quite active and the slag trains appeared to be operating but there didn't seem to be much happening on the through lines. A short investigative walk soon revealed why for there had been a most spectacular derailment of one of the loaded tube trains on the curve coming down from Weldon Road bridge. Literally every wagon was off the rails and some had toppled over spilling their load onto the ballast. At first glance it appeared that clearing it all up would be a real major job requiring several days but there was a well organised permanent way gang who had the assistance of a mobile rail mounted crane, so when I next went down there again, not long after, it was once again business as normal as though nothing had happened.

On another occasion a lunch time visit to the Tarmac Plant saw one of the 56 class RSH's come rolling down from beneath Stanion Lane bridge with a loaded ironstone train and then halted at the water tower for a fill up. Whilst this was going on, I could hear the sound of shovelling in the cab and also it was obvious that the blower was on as indicated by the vertical column of black smoke rising vertically upwards from the chimney. Having filled the tank the driver made a vigorous but clean start with no slipping but to my slight surprise made no attempt to ease off as the train picked up speed around the curve following the water tower. In fact he kept it working really hard and as it disappeared under Weldon Road bridge the column of black smoke had to be seen to be believed, as did the noise coming from the engine. There was a brief silence as they passed under the bridge but it must have literally burst out the other side, first as a huge cloud of black

The lorries in the background are a clue to the location. No. 6 was seen between duties in 1966, a year before it was finally withdrawn. The sheds in the left background are part of the tube works complex.

smoke and then getting farther away (but not any quieter) with a tall column of white steam mixing in with the general blackness. It honestly looked like a miniature mobile volcano, it really did. The driver kept this up all the way past the big tube works sheds and even as the train curved round behind the Lancs & Corby sheds it was still possible to follow its progress from the trail of smoke and the noise. Eventually it all faded into the distance and peace descended but I have often since wondered what inspired the driver to work his engine in such an energetic manner. The subsequent comings and goings of the tube works engines seemed a bit tame after that!

No. 62 gets away from a water stop with a loaded iron ore train in November 1968, this picture was taken on the occasion referred to above. The track here looks as though it has been subject to re-ballasting and re-sleepering.

A driver's eye view from No.13 as it gets a heavy train on the move, as another train of empty slag wagons passes over the flyover on its way back to the blast furnaces. The valve on the steam dome was used on the oil fired engines to provide a steam supply to the bunker and the burners, but on No. 13 it wasn't connected as it was coal fired. The upper surfaces of the engine are well splattered with particles of grit and grime that were such a feature of this place.

On the left, No. 21 is the Tarmac Plant shunter as No. 18 departs the scene light engine having delivered some empty wagons, whilst above on the viaduct one of the English Electric diesels returns a train of empty slag tipping wagons to the blast furnace area.

No. 21 shunts the newly arrived wagons back into the sidings.

More shunting operations with No.21 as No.63 arrives on the scene. Having run downhill to the Stanion Lane Bridge, its driver has just opened the regulator to accelerate the train ready for the climb up to the Weldon Road bridge and beyond.

And finally No. 63's driver is obviously not planning to stop for water at the Tarmac Plant as the train is accelerated away from the scene.

A busy 1966 scene at the viaduct, an unidentified 56 Class with a loaded iron ore train passes No. 7 on permanent way duties and No.6 which is working the Tarmac sidings.

Two pictures of the same engine at the same location. No. 20 was regularly allocated to the tube works and in the upper August 1967 picture, on what was clearly an overcast day, it is seen working hard heading for the south exchange sidings with a train of loaded tube wagons.

The lower view in contrast was on a very hot July day in the same year with the engine returning from the exchange sidings with a load of empty long wheel base wagons. Two of the crew can be seen half hanging out the cab in an attempt to keep cool. Stanion Lane bridge is in the background.

A very clean No.23 causes a minor traffic hold-up as it delivers a train of the ubiquitous 16 ton mineral wagons to the tarmac sidings in 1966.

The ballasting gang are at work as No. 58 passes by wrong line in July 1967. The engine is in the process of crossing over to the correct running lines and the shunter can be seen standing on the running plate, no doubt ready to clamber up and grasp the hose when the train stops to take on water.

Having just passed under Stanion Lane bridge, No.45 *Colwyn* is seen approaching the tarmac plant with a loaded iron ore train bound for the works. February 1968.

A crisp November 1967 Saturday morning sees No. 38 *Dolobran* hurrying past the tarmac plant with a lightweight permanent way train on its way back to Pen Green.

And no sooner was *Dolobran* receding in the distance than No.22 arrives down from the works with a short train of demountable hopper wagons.

On the same day as the two preceding pictures, No.16 passes the tarmac sidings with a loaded train of tubes for delivery to the south exchange sidings.

Against a background of a multitude of electricity transmission lines, No.7 is at work in the tarmac sidings. It appears that some of the graded slag products, rather than being loaded into railway wagons, have actually been deposited on top of the saddle tank and cab. The canary yellow livery was never applied to these older engines but despite the aura of neglect, these Barclays always evoked an image of solid, reliable competence, even when 65 years old. November 1967.

"Pre-Austerity" No.3 from Glendon East during its short time at Corby, about to pass under Stanion Lane bridge with a train of empties destined for either Cowthick or the Oakley branches. This engine is another example of the historic pre-Austerities. June 1967.

Swirling smoke partly obscures a busy scene at Stanion Lane bridge, with trains passing by in both directions. No.20 is following a short distance behind with another train heading up towards the South Exchange sidings whilst on the opposite track is yet another delivery of empty mineral wagons destined for somewhere in the works. No.20 is obviously going well as it attacks the gradient and it can be imagined that its driver is hoping the train in front will also maintain satisfactory progress and not bring everything to a stop. October 1969.

Track maintenance was facilitated by the use of mobile cranes and in this 1966 view No. 7 is shown with one of the machines manufactured by the well known firm of Thomas Smith's of Rodley near Leeds. The cranes were extensively used and it was not at all unusual to see them either in use or being moved about the site.

Major track work being carried out in the cutting west of Stanion Lane Bridge, one of the busiest parts of the whole system. Notice the traffic light colour signal on the left and in the distance the junction for the Cowthick and Oakley quarry lines. May 1969.

Seen here in March 1969 at the tarmac plant with No.18 is the permanent way train. Its appearance was quite random and unpredictable although there must surely have been some sort of planned schedule for it. The number of wagons in the train seemed to vary but it always included the blue ex-BR van. Immediately to the left of the van is the spire of Corby Parish church and on the right background the white houses are situated on Weldon Road itself.

No.13 having just emerged from the Tarmac Plant building in December 1967. By this time the elderly Andrew Barclays had been replaced by the Hawthorn Leslies.

The oldest of the raised firebox Manning Wardles, dating from 1910, was No.38 *Dolobran* and in contrast to the elderly Barclays it was still very smartly turned out. Usually allocated to the minerals department permanent way train, it was still obviously capable of working a heavy iron ore train when required. The black and yellow striped device appears to have been intended as a safety aid but was eventually removed. It is seen here passing the tarmac plant and heading for the Weldon Road bridge in 1966.

Two pictures as a reminder of a gloomy winter's day. No.18 has just arrived from the iron and steel works with a train of vans and, having run round them, is setting off for the south exchange sidings, whilst in the lower picture No. 13 was busy shunting the Tarmac Plant sidings.

With a nod towards the famous artist J.M.W. Turner, the lower picture could perhaps be entitled 'Fog, Grime, Grit and Smoke' with possibly 'Cold' added too. We might well have wished that it was sunny July and the location was out in the countryside around Harringworth but by March 1970 steam activity at Corby was greatly reduced and to see these two engines at work was quite a bonus.

Left. With a sharp exhaust and lifting safety valves, No.20 makes an energetic restart with what appears to be a loaded tube train after having stopped for water. Anyone who has ever experienced a footplate ride on the average industrial loco will know that it is not usually a Rolls-Royce experience, but a careful look at some of the undulations in the track in this picture will perhaps offer an explanation of why this is so. March 1969.

Below. Work stained No. 13 was on Tarmac Plant shunting duties in March 1969. Track maintenance work is in progress in the background.

8. WELDON ROAD BRIDGES

One of the Weldon Road bridges was near the tube works main road entrance, just under a ten minute walk from our office in the direction of Weldon village. It was a favourite location for photographs as it was on a busy part of the railway and inbound trains faced a very stiff climb. On a fine day it was a most agreeable spot to spend a lunch break as some sort of action was almost guaranteed. It was possible to look down to the Tarmac Plant where it might be possible to catch a distant glimpse of the resident shunting engine at work. A little further over was the flyover that carried the slag trains over the lines that went up to the south exchange sidings so there might be a bit of activity there too. Trains inbound to the works, either tube empties or loaded with iron ore became visible as they emerged from under the flyover, then it would be a choice of either a stop to take on water or a run through. Through trains had the advantage of momentum, but stop or not, on the approach to the bridge, as the gradient steepened with any sort of train the engine was having to work seriously hard. The second of the Weldon Road bridges was that nearest Corby village, and regularly used by trains conveying slag from the blast furnaces to the slag bank. These trains were invariably diesel hauled and although other steam hauled trains did put in an appearance they were quite spasmodic. However, when returning from evening lectures at technical college sometimes there would be a modest degree of interest here if one of the slag trains was passing beneath. In our safety conscious era it seems unbelievable that such trains would be allowed to pass beneath a public road bridge with just a normal height parapet but back then it was possible to lean over slightly and be literally directly above the contents of the wagons, sometimes bright orange, sometimes dull red, but always extremely hot, and see it splashing and rippling as the train clattered its way over the rail joints. After 55 years I was actually wondering if my memory was accurate but a Google Street View image and indeed a more recent visit showed that the bridge was exactly where I remembered it to be and the parapets remain just as they were. This stretch of line is now lifted but it would be interesting to scramble down to the track bed and see if there are any lumps of solidified material that had been spilt from the passing trains.

No.19 was often allocated to the tube works and is seen here somewhat unusually with an inbound train of bogie bolster wagons with what appears to be a delivery of constructional beams. In the background can be seen the environs of the tarmac plant whilst on the extreme right is the flyover used for slag deliveries. On the original print the black smoke appears to be coming from the tarmac plant shunting engine. 14th April 1967.

This viewpoint from the other side of the bridge looking towards the tube works illustrates the steepness of the gradient faced by trains returning to the works. The wagons in the background are at the eastern end of the tube works sidings. The engine is No. 12 and the train setting out for the south exchange sidings appears to be composed mainly of long wheel base tube wagons with a pair of bogie bolsters in the middle.

Adjacent to the bridge on the downhill side was a siding serving a number of fuel oil tanks. Minerals department No.35 and the permanent way train was stabled there for a short time on the 22nd December 1966. I was fortunate to have my camera on this occasion as this engine was quite elusive to photograph, likely to just turn up and then disappear again.

A lengthy iron ore train hauled by No. 62 and banked by No. 53. April 1967.

No.64 approaches the Weldon Bridge with a loaded iron ore train bound for the works in November 1967. A careful examination of this picture shows that it is being banked by the Yorkshire Engine Company 8-coupled diesel and hence has probably come from Oakley quarries. The massive tarmac plant building dominated the railway scene around here.

November 1967 and No. 20 doesn't appear to be in the best of condition and was making hard work of a train of empty wagons destined for the tube works.

No. 21 was also a regular on tube works duties and is seen here being driven enthusiastically, returning from the south exchange sidings with a delivery of empties. Given the speed of the engine I would imagine the ride on the footplate would be quite lively! Affixed to the rear of the bunker is a long handled shovel carried by most of the iron and steel works engines at Corby which was principally used for cleaning ashes from out of the ash pan.

No. 40 was a slightly special engine in that in the whole time of my association with Corby I saw it very rarely as it seemed to be always working within the confines of the works, rarely venturing outside. Its history was also different from the remainder of the Hawthorn Leslies as it dated from 1919 and was second hand to Corby, being transferred there in 1931. Here are two pictures of it with an empty inbound train of tube wagons in 1967.

No. 59 on a loaded iron ore train passing one of the English Electric diesels which is on an outbound train. The tarmac plant looms in the background. April 1967.

A full load and a steep gradient, obviously working hard but still a bit of steam to spare at the safety valves, No.57 with a loaded iron ore train destined for the North Bank reception sidings. A cold December day but well worth waiting for. December 1967.

This is a view of the railway at the 'other' Weldon Road bridge that was used by the slag trains and this is one of the random steam workings referred to above. Nos. 22 and 58 are passing by at not much more than a walking pace, both heading in the direction of the blast furnaces which can be seen in the background. No. 58 is light engine whilst No. 22 has a short train of assorted wagons, nearest the engine is a standard mineral wagon, followed by a tank wagon labelled BENZENE (one of the coke oven by-products) and then an internal user iron ore wagon. It was most unusual indeed to see one of the quarry engines along this stretch and one can only speculate as to its destination.

Always expect the unexpected! This is a slightly unusual working in that No. 39 *Rhos* is propelling a longish works train passing the Tube Works adjacent to Weldon Road. In the late 1960s this engine appeared to be used exclusively on works or permanent way trains but it was always a pleasure to see as it was so obviously different from the other engines in the minerals fleet.

Against a background of the coke oven's chimneys, No.23 and the permanent way gang slowly make their way back to the works. After the demise of the Barclays and the transfer away of *Wellingborough* No.3 for a time this engine was regularly used on p-way duties.

Looking towards the blast furnaces from the 'other' Weldon Road bridge in April 1971 with No.20 making its way light engine towards the iron and steel works. The bridge spanning the tracks was made by Tubewrights Ltd., a Stewarts and Lloyds owned company. The right hand set of tracks, used by trains en-route to the tarmac plant slag tipping bank, are fitted with a double set of checkrails, a safety feature to guard against derailments?

9. PEN GREEN SHED

For us Pen Green shed was the focal point of the railways serving the ironstone quarries. It was easily accessible from Gretton Brook Road and all inbound trains from the Harringworth direction passed very close by. The shed itself was a large modern structure, 4 bays, 8 roads in total, capable of holding all of the engines with a little space inside to spare. Very good for interior photographs but the downside of having such a spacious building was that until the time of mass withdrawals engines were not usually left outside. Hence any speculative Sunday afternoon photographers were thwarted because there was nothing of interest to see, in contrast perhaps to other locations such as Irchester or Blisworth or Nassington. This area was above the Kettering to Manton line Corby Tunnel and photographs taken around the Gretton Brook Road level crossing sometimes feature a tunnel ventilator in the background. Trains from the Weldon direction, either Priors Hall North or Priors Hall South, and Oakley/Cowthick entered the works by a slightly different route to the south which by-passed the shed area.

Late on a Saturday morning would see the trains pass through on their way to the North Bank reception sidings, some being top and tailed, others with just a single engine. Later the engines would reappear at the shed for the time honoured disposal procedure, tanks filled up, injector gurgling away, fire dropped, ashes cleaned out. And then one by one, with the merest wisp of steam and with no more sound than the ticking of a grandfather clock they would be shuffled into the shed and put away. The shutters would come down and that would be that until our next free Saturday. Happy days.

Day's work done, Nos. 56 and 57 stand outside at Pen Green awaiting their turn to be put away inside. February 1968.

4 bays, 8 roads, one by one the engines have been put away, the shutters pulled down and silence descended. When the shed was busy there was a real atmosphere here but as can be deduced from this picture once everyone had gone home there was little to see outside apart from the odd heap of smouldering ashes.

A frosty November Saturday morning and as the engines finished their shift this board indicated where they were to be stabled in the shed. On this particular day 7 of them had been out and in use.

Heaps of smoking cinders indicate that the fires have been thrown out and these two are almost ready to be put away inside the shed. This was once an occurrence on scores of industrial railways up and down the country and part of the routine. July 1967.

Unfortunately the rapid large scale deployment of the ex-British Railways Class 14 diesels quickly ensured the redundancy of the steam fleet and so the environs of Pen Green were eventually blighted by the familiar sight of rows of unwanted engines.

However all was not lost as several of them found their way into the preservation movement, the '56' class engines in particular being perceived as being especially suitable.

For the industrial enthusiast the interior of Pen Green was an almost other world existence and certainly not the usual industrial loco shed experience. No leaky roofs or bricked up or missing windows and no narrow cramped spaces cluttered with all the paraphernalia necessary to keep engines in service. Instead it was bright and airy, neat and tidy, and had ample space to see everything properly with room to spare. This despite the fact that we had already seen those self same engines half an hour earlier as they arrived with their trainloads of iron ore. The environment was more like a main line engine shed as was found in many of the larger towns in the country during the steam age. Perhaps the only slight downside was that all the engines were more or less standardised but we were quite happy to go along with that.

One particular memory is of a cold damp winter's day when all the engines had been brought in and the roller shutters closed down. For us the still warm engines were an impromptu source of central heating and we were most reluctant to let go of this cosy atmosphere. Once indoors there is a special ambience about engines cooling down, heat haze above the chimney, an occasional wisp of escaping steam, the sound of dripping water, and the pervading smell of hot oil. There was a realisation that the end of steam was imminent and once the engines finally finished work then scenes such as this would be gone for ever. But all good things come to an end and eventually it was time to exit through the side door and rejoin the real world and our ride home, gloomy and miserable as it was.

Two scenes inside Pen Green taken in early 1968. Engine in the lower picture is No.45 *Colwyn*.

No. 45 *Colwyn* was an engine that I used to see very regularly and here it is again, drawn up behind No.52. This is in direct contrast to one of the iron and steelworks engines, No. 40, which I only saw a very few times during the whole of my association with the railways at Corby. April 1968.

Bright winter sunshine lights up No.57.

And finally the future has arrived at Pen Green. Steam has finished and diesels are now the order of the day. This picture shows a trio of the type 14 or D95xx Swindon built diesel hydraulics in the company of one of the physically much smaller Rolls-Royce machines. August 1969.

10. THE QUARRY BRANCHES

A network of country lanes lies between Corby and Harringworth and some of these crossed over some of the branch lines that connected the quarries and the works. One Saturday morning routine involved starting at Weldon, crossing as many bridges as possible and looking out to see if any trains were in the vicinity. Not all of the branches were in use all of the time but we usually managed to see some steam activity during the course of our perambulation. If we saw something coming it was a scramble to park the bikes, remove crash helmets, empty duffle bags, set up the camera and a find suitable 'spot' for a picture. Then it was on to the next bridge until we eventually arrived at Pen Green.

There was also a branch running alongside Gretton Brook Road to Earlstrees quarry, actually passing through the remains of a farmyard in the process. This is shown on maps as Gretton Brook Farm. Along some of its length this railway was separated from the road by a hedge and it was quite frustrating to see one of the trains passing by literally yards away but not to be able to take photographs because of the profusion of bushes. One particular wet and dark winters morning just as we arrived we could see a dim and distant light coming down the line but we couldn't make out quite what it was. Finally it materialised out of the murk and gloom as one of the Kitsons, slowly making its way down the Earlstrees branch in the darkness, its way 'illuminated' by a single oil lamp on the front of the engine.

The trains serving Cowthick and Oakley quarries, to the south of Corby, ran past the tarmac plant before branching off on their own separate lines. A further item of interest was the overhead cable way that connected Oakley sidings with quarries at Rothwell about 5 miles away.

Trains from the Weldon direction, usually either from Priors Hall North or Priors Hall South quarries entered the works by a slightly different route to the south which bypassed the shed area.

The quarries were a potentially hazardous environment as in some locations the iron ore was 80 or more feet below the surface and as the quarry face advanced all this overlying strata was removed and deposited to one side. Given the depth of the cut and the height of the deposited spoil the quarries seemed much deeper than they actually were.

During my works employee introduction we were taken out to see one of the draglines that were used for this task. It is difficult to describe the scale of these machines, the body of which would have encompassed a reasonable sized block of flats, the jib, or boom, that carried the bucket was about 300 feet long, and the bucket itself had a capacity of nearly 30 cubic yards. When travelling around the countryside around Corby the huge jibs of these machines, poking out above the spoil heaps, became almost a characteristic feature of the landscape. One dark winters evening whilst cycling back to Weldon after technical college evening classes I happened to pause at the Weldon Road bridge to see if there were any passing trains. As it happened there wasn't but the draglines in both Oakley and Cowthick pits were still at work and could be seen clearly in the distance. The jibs were equipped with searchlights to illuminate the working space and placed right on top of the jib was a red warning light. It was fascinating to watch the pair of them swinging rhythmically to and fro, scooping up the overburden and depositing it on the other side of pit, with the bright lights illuminating the darkness. Then turning away towards Weldon I realised that the Priors Hall machine was also working away, again rhythmically describing bright arcs in the night sky. So in the sweep of an eye all three draglines could be seen, a very visual reminder of just how much effort was required to actually get the iron ore from out of the ground.

An engine driver's eye view of Priors Hall North face in November 1968. The excavator to the left is a loading shovel used for filling the wagons whilst the Dragline is the Ransomes and Rapier W1400 which, when new, was the largest walking dragline in the world. The two black dots immediately to the left of the machine are in fact people.

A water supply was provided at Deene Bottom at the entrance to the Priors Hall North workings. No.64 is departing for the works with a loaded train whilst No. 47 *Carnarvon* waits in the siding with a train of empties.

Later on the same day, No. 47 *Carnarvon* now has the task of moving one of the dragline buckets on a bogie well wagon.

The flagman at Gretton Brook Road railway crossing holds out his red flag as a loaded train heads towards the works. Most of the railway workers were usually benignly disposed to us young enthusiasts but just once at this place we had a surprise. Whilst we were waiting at the trackside by the crossing, the flagman came out, scowled at us and greeted us with the words "I'll be bl**dy glad when steam has finished!" With that he saw the train safely across and stalked back to his cabin. He was soon to be granted his wish as shortly afterwards the first of the ex-BR diesels began to arrive and before long steam was indeed finished. December 1967.

An overcast day in July 1967 sees No.57 near Gretton on an inbound train, this is looking towards the steep escarpment overlooking the Welland Valley that the railway follows all the way to Harringworth. Although obviously hauling a substantial load and working hard, the engine has steam to spare. We had some time to prepare for this picture and I was able to scramble to the top of a spoil heap to achieve a panoramic view of the scene.

Also photographed in July 1967 on a perfect summer's day deep in the countryside and well away from the environs of Corby, No.53 is pushing a loaded train towards Harringworth sidings. The shunter can be seen riding on the leading wagon ready to jump down and set the points for the correct reception track. In the distance are Dryleas Wood and Hollow Wood, coppices that are a feature of what remains of Rockingham Forest in this area of Northamptonshire.

Priors Hall quarry had two outlets, the southern one passing close to Weldon village. This June 1967 picture shows pre-Austerity No.3 during its temporary allocation at Corby at work on a loaded train. As previously mentioned, this engine was one of the batch destined for the proposed Islip railway but instead went to the Stanton Ironworks Company at Glendon East quarries, eventually making a brief visit to Corby 26 years later. After the closure of the railway system, this cutting was widened and now forms part of the Weldon A43 by-pass.

No. 46 *Cardigan* near Harringworth, the railway here runs on the top of the ironstone bed whilst in the side of the cutting several other strata layers are revealed. The tracks in the quarries were continually re-aligned and moved as the working face advanced so these works trains could be seen widely over all parts of the system. July 1967.

The day's activities nearly done, Nos. 64 and 62 are coasting downhill and approaching Gretton Brook Road level crossing in April 1968. Judging by the discolouration, No. 64's smokebox door has got seriously hot sometime in the recent past. This area is on top of the Kettering to Manton line Corby Tunnel.

In contrast to the Stewarts and Lloyds railway at Gretton Brook Road which at the Corby tunnel actually passed above the Kettering to Manton railway line, near the village of Great Oakley it ran under it at the Harpers Brook viaduct. The Oakley quarry branch sidings were located within sight of the viaduct where on a hot summer's scorching day in 1969, No.59 was seen filling up with water ready for the run back to Corby with a loaded train.

An extra source of traffic on the Oakley branch was the overhead ropeway that extended to quarries near Rothwell, a distance of about 5 miles. Unlike a railway the ropeway could largely ignore features on the ground and follow a direct route. In these pictures taken on the 18th May 1964 it appears to dominate the local landscape but its working lifespan was destined to be quite short, from 1959 to 1966. Wherever the ropeway crossed a public highway, as a safeguard against any malfunctions in its operation, gantry style bridges were provided. The one shown was situated on the Rushton to Corby road with the view looking towards Storefield Wood.

In August 1969 the system was out of use and the buckets had been removed. This is the old A6 road crossing looking towards Desborough. A few months later the system was dismantled.

When not in use the ropeway buckets were stored in this facility near the Oakley branch. It was located in old quarry workings and even though overgrown the old ironstone face can still be seen in the background.

No. 64 with a loaded train near Weldon on the Priors Hall branch on a hot July day in 1967, very good for the lineside photographer, not so comfortable for those on the footplate.

The line to Earlstrees quarry ran parallel to Gretton Brook Road which is immediately behind the hedgerow. In doing so it passed by some old agricultural barns of what was once Gretton Brook Farm, parts of which are seen here. Pictured in November 1968 as No 47 *Carnarvon* was delivering a train of empties.

Has the present-day health and safety culture ruled out the possibility of events such as this ever happening again? Clambering up ladders into open wagons, straw bales as seats, breezing through the open air and being showered in smuts and cinders, whilst being wreathed in a thick, damp mist. Held on 11th January 1969 and tinged with great sadness, a special railtour to mark the end of steam in the quarries at Corby was topped and tailed by Nos. 56 and No.44 *Conway* to Wakerley and back.

11. POSTSCRIPT

Most of the preceeding colour pictures were taken on Kodachrome film which was available in cassettes allowing 24 or 36 exposures. 36 exposure was the preferred option but pecuniary pressures ensured that many of my films were of the 24 exposure variety. An incidental advantage of this was that film would be used more quickly and results would be available sooner. Kodak slides were mounted in cardboard surrounds which during processing were date stamped and numbered according to the position on the film. This was extremely useful many years later when determining the order in which pictures were taken. When films were returned from processing I always annotated them according to subject and location, but the dates quoted in the text are usually the month in which the film was actually processed. However, given the actual rate at which we used the film and the speed of processing these dates are not so far from when the pictures were actually taken.